Why Cucumbers Are Better Than Men

By The Cucumber Group

M. L. Brooks
Donna E. Hanbery
Ivor Matz
Tam and Craig Westover

Illustrated by Risa Glickman

M. EVANS AND COMPANY, INC.
New York

Library of Congress Cataloging in Publication Data
Main entry under title:

Why cucumbers are better than men.

   1. Men—Anecdotes, facetiae, satire, etc. I. Brooks,
M. L. II. Cucumber Group.
HQ1090.W49   1983   305.3'1   82-24194

ISBN 0-87131-399-5

M. Evans and Company, Inc.
216 East 49 Street
New York, New York 10017

Design by Diane Gedymin

Manufactured in the United States of America

9 8 7 6 5 4 3 2

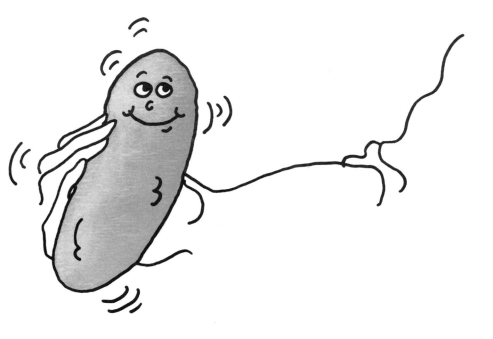

Cucumbers are better than men because . . .

Cucumbers are easy to pick up.

You can fondle a cucumber in the supermarket . . .
    and you know how firm it is *before* you take it home.

With cucumbers, you'll never find used jogging shorts in your lingerie drawer.

A cucumber won't charge your birthday present on your account.

Cucumbers won't tell you how to vote.

Cucumbers won't use the last of the ice cubes and not fill the trays.

Your cucumber will never enlist, get drafted, or threaten to join the French Foreign Legion.

A cucumber will never introduce you as "just a friend."

Cucumbers don't make you cry.

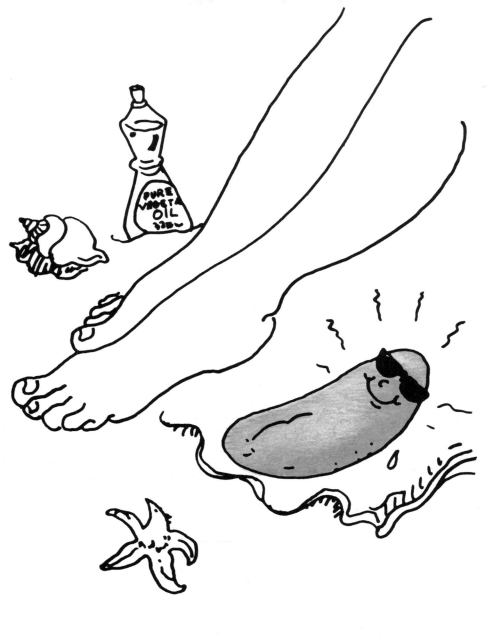

Cucumbers can get away any weekend.

A cucumber won't ask, "Am I the first?"

Cucumbers don't care if you're a virgin.

Cucumbers won't tell other cucumbers you're a virgin.

Cucumbers won't tell anyone you're not a virgin anymore.

With cucumbers, you don't have to be a virgin more than once.

———————————

Cucumbers won't write your name and number on the men's room wall.

Cucumbers won't tell you a vasectomy will ruin it for them.

Cucumbers won't make you wear kinky clothes or go to bed with your boots on.

Cucumbers aren't into chains and leather, talking dirty, or swinging with fruits and nuts.

You only eat cucumber when you feel like it.

———————————

You can have as many cucumbers as you can handle.

Cucumbers don't notice your roots.

Cucumbers don't care if *everyone* else notices your roots.

Cucumbers never ask your age.

Cucumbers don't care if you're jailbait.

Cucumbers won't lose your apartment keys at the YMCA.

A cucumber won't tell you size doesn't count.

Cucumbers are never too tired, too old, or too bad.

Cucumbers can't carry colds . . .
    and cucumbers grow their own penicillin.

A cucumber won't try to tell you natural childbirth is best because painkillers are bad for you.

———————————

A cucumber won't mind hiding in the refrigerator when your mother comes over.

Cucumbers aren't jealous of your gynecologist, ski instructor, or hairdresser.

A cucumber won't want to join your support group.

A cucumber never wants to improve your mind.

Cucumbers aren't into meaningful discussions.

Cucumbers won't ask about your last lover . . .
    or speculate about your next one.

A cucumber will never make a scene because there are other cucumbers in the refrigerator.

———————————

Cucumbers can handle rejection.

A cucumber won't pout if you have a headache.

A cucumber won't care what time of the month it is.

A cucumber won't give it up for Lent.

With a cucumber, you never have to say you're sorry.

———————————

A cucumber never wants to get it on when your nails
are wet.

A cucumber doesn't care if you don't shave your legs.

Cucumbers don't have five o'clock shadow.

Cucumbers don't care if you have a zit.

Cucumbers don't leave whisker burns, fall asleep on your chest, or drool on the pillow.

A cucumber will never give you a hickey.

Afterward, a cucumber won't . . .
    want to shake hands and be friends.
    say, "I'll call you a cab."
    leave you wondering for a month.
    tell you he's not the marrying kind.
    tell you he *is* the marrying kind.
    call his mother, ex-wife, or therapist.
    take you to confession.

Cucumbers are still good when they're pickled.

Cucumbers won't wear your clothes, your makeup, or your underwear.

Cucumbers will never make your living room smell like beer, sweat, and cigars.

Cucumbers never say "oops."

Cucumbers won't switch the station on your radio, return your car on empty, or smoke your last cigarette.

A cucumber won't switch channels from your "soap" to *All-Star Wrestling*.

A cucumber will never call you by the wrong name.

———————————

Cucumbers never answer your phone or borrow your car.

A cucumber won't eat all your food or drink all your liquor.

Cucumbers won't use up all your laundry change playing poker.

———————————

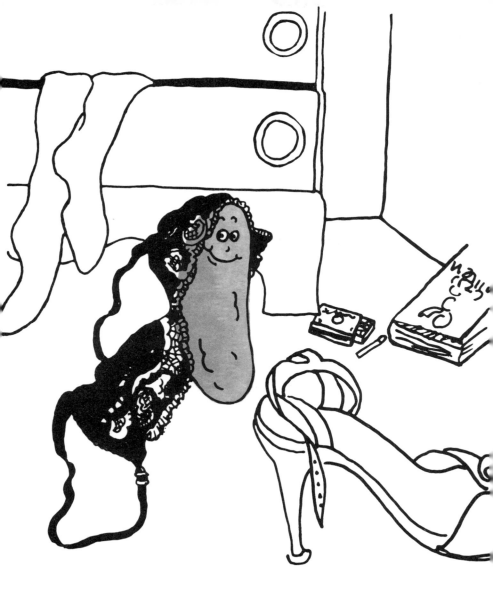

A cucumber won't mind if your room is a mess.

Cucumbers will never ask, "What's a nice girl like you doing in a supermarket like this?"

Cucumbers aren't into astrology. When your best friend totals your car, your rent goes up, you gain ten pounds, and your parakeet dies, a cucumber will never tell you, "Uranus is conjunct your moon. Next week will be worse."

Cucumbers don't have etchings.

Cucumbers are never cranky in the morning. But you can be.

Cucumbers don't eat crackers in bed—or care if you do.

Cucumbers don't have chemistry.

Cucumbers never hand you a line.

Cucumbers don't have sharp toenails and dull minds.

———————————

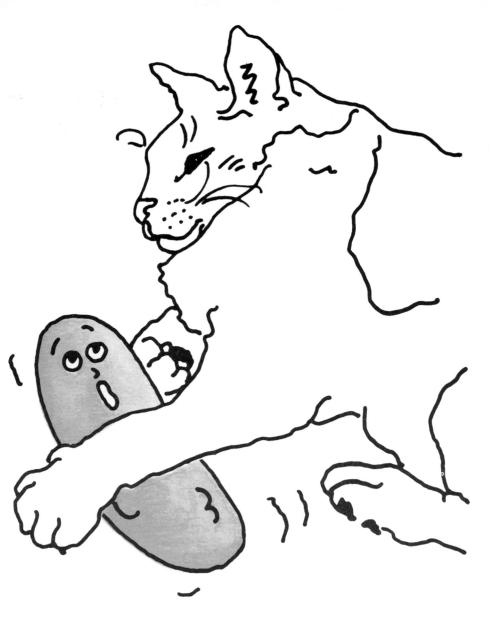

A cucumber isn't allergic to your cat.

Cucumbers are cheap.

Cucumbers don't have a bald spot.

Cucumbers don't beg to come over to dinner.

Cucumbers always give their all.

You don't have to give your cucumber a birthday party.

A cucumber doesn't turn your bathroom into a library.

Cucumbers won't go through your medicine chest.

Cucumbers won't leave hair in the sink or a ring in the tub.

Cucumbers don't leave dirty shorts on the floor.

A cucumber never forgets to flush the toilet.

A cucumber doesn't flush the toilet while you're taking a shower.

With a cucumber, the toilet seat is always the way you left it.

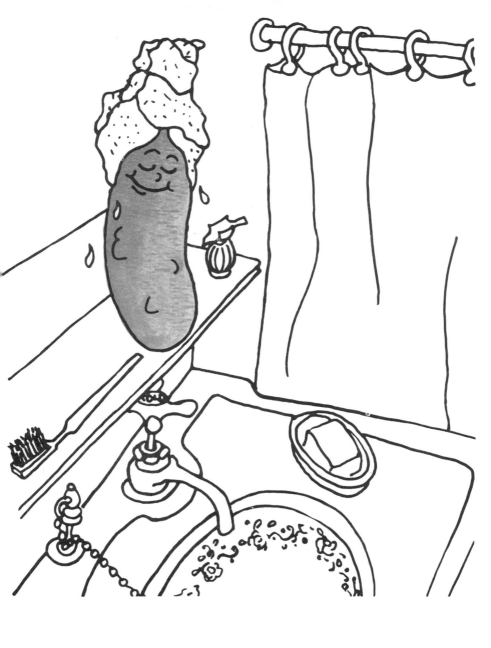

A cucumber doesn't use your toothbrush, roll-on, cr hair spray.

Cucumbers don't . . .
>ask, "What's for dinner?" the minute you get home from work.
>want to know your vital statistics.
>run up long-distance phone bills.
>fight about money.
>have mothers.
>bum cigarettes.
>take you home for Christmas.

———————

A cucumber never has to call "the wife."

Cucumbers don't have mid-life crises.

A cucumber won't leave you for a cheerleader or an ex-nun.

Cucumbers don't play the guitar and try to find themselves.

You won't find out later that your cucumber . . .
>is married.
>likes you—but loves your sister . . . or your brother.

———————

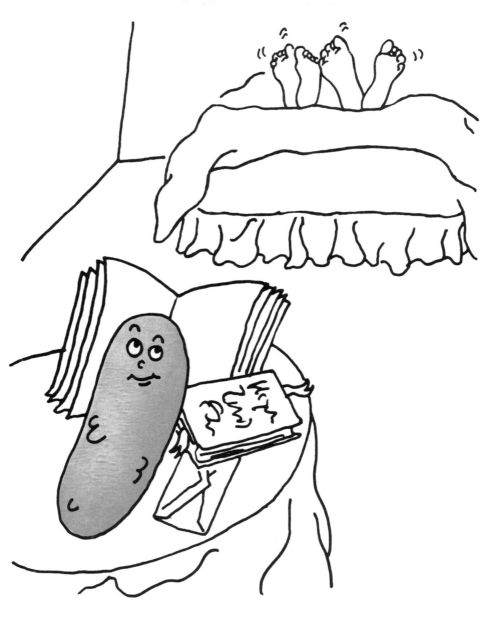

Cucumbers don't expect you to be faithful.

A cucumber won't work your crossword puzzle with ink.

With a cucumber, you don't have to play Florence Nightingale during the flu season.

———————————————

A cucumber doesn't have softball practice on the day you move.

Cucumbers never tell you what they did on R & R.

A cucumber won't ask for a transfer just when you're up for a promotion.

A cucumber won't wear a leisure suit to your office Christmas party.

You don't have to wait until halftime to talk to your cucumber.

A cucumber won't take you to a disco and dump you for a flashy outfit.

———————————————

You can take your cucumber on the road.

A cucumber doesn't care if you always spend the holidays with your family.

A cucumber won't ask to be put through med school.

A cucumber won't tell you he's outgrown you intellectually.

Cucumbers never expect you to have little cucumbers.

Cucumbers don't say, "Let's keep trying until we have a boy."

A cucumber won't insist the little cukes be raised Catholic, Jewish, or Orthodox Vegetarian.

———————

Cucumbers don't expect a home-cooked dinner.

When you bend over, a cucumber won't sneak a peek down your blouse.

Cucumbers won't make you bleach your mustache.

———————

You can take your cucumber with a dash of salt.

A cucumber won't read your diary.

You'll never catch your cucumber demanding breakfast in bed.

The cucumber you love will never ask to be fixed up with your sister, your best friend, or your girl scout troop.

With a cucumber, you can keep your name, your credit, and your career.

A cucumber will never contest a divorce, demand a property settlement, or seek custody of *anything*.

Cucumbers won't . . .
> floss when you're trying to get in the mood.
> point out the dust on the shelf you can't reach.
> play connect-the-dots with your freckles.
> practice karate with your bookshelves.
> pick their teeth at the dinner table.
> leave size thirteen wing tips for you to trip over.
> adjust the car seat so you can't reach the pedals.
> put hot peppers on your half of the pizza.
> make *you* go to the drugstore.

Cucumbers don't care if you make more money than they do.

A cucumber won't compare you to a centerfold.

Cucumbers can't count to ten.

Cucumbers don't tell you they liked you better with long hair.

A cucumber will never leave you . . .
    for another woman . . .
    for another man . . .
    for another cucumber.

A cucumber will never call and say, "I have to work late, honey," and then come home smelling like another woman.

A cucumber never snaps your bra, pinches your butt, or gives you a snuggy.

You always know where your cucumber has been.

A cucumber won't leave town on New Year's Eve.

You can go to a movie with a cucumber—and see the movie.

At a drive-in, you can stay in the front seat.

A cucumber can always wait until you get home.

A cucumber won't drag you to a John Wayne film festival.

Cucumbers never need a round of applause.

Cucumbers won't ask:
    "Am I the best?"
    "How was it?"

With a cucumber you can get a single room . . .
    and you won't have to check in as "Mrs. Cucumber."

A cucumber will always respect you in the morning.

A cucumber won't eat all the popcorn . . . or send you out for Milk Duds.

It's easy to drop a cucumber.